Bits of Yesterday

Bits of Yesterday

Mary Elizabeth Bailey

To order additional copies of this book, contact:
Xlibris Corporation
1-888-795-4274
www.Xlibris.com
Orders@Xlibris.com
56949

Contents

Dedication

To John, David, Barbara and Janice
For All Their Help and Love.

Family

My wonderful family

Looking Back

Written for the Bell family reunion—July 1997

Looking back is good.
It's understood
That we should
Explore the rambling roads of the past
But—not—too—fast.

For we might miss
In doing this
The charming churchyards
Here and there scattered,
Wind and rain battered;
They mattered
To those who sleep so quietly
Unaware
Of stories told in stone,
And we might not see
The little church there alone.

No—not too fast.
We might not hear
The school bell of a yesteryear
Ringing—clear.
We might miss the school,
Bulwark of the golden rule,
Where ink well eyes of ancient desks
Lined row on row
Just so,
Bring back the sounds of quill pens
Scratching—to and fro.

And moving too fast,
How could we feel
Emotions very real
Of those long gone?
"Prudence—May, 1890-1890, June"
So soon!
Some mother's terrible tears
Felt all those years
For a child who hardly was.

It is good—this looking back
To stalwart souls who tramped the mellow plains
And made with aid of sun and rains
An almost Eden.
For you and I are a part of what we were;
All—arbiters of what we could become
When all is said and done.

A *Child* Is Born

Into the sterile stillness, ruby red
He came, announcing shrilly he was there,
And massive hands reached out. His little head
Diminutive was held with infinite care.

Oh—he was so loved that little something new,
Sticky wetness glistening in the light,
Life-line trailing out behind, askew,
Before the scissors came—decisive bite.

Tiny wrinkled hands flailed out in space,
Old man's eyes surveyed the great unknown.
Unbidden came a smile upon his face
Almost as if he had already grown.

And God looked down again and called it good;
When I held this child I understood.

Ann

Four Christmases you have been gone,
But we can see you still,
With golden hair and glowing face.
And eyes alight with thrill.

There's a little glimpse of mischief
In your face we still perceive
As you sit cross legged on the floor
Wrapping, Christmas Eve

You loved to wear your Christmas plaid
And holly on your blouse;
The sounds of carols that you played,
Would permeate the house.

And every ornament you made
Displayed your special touch,
For each was worked with tender care
And each was loved so much.

Four Christmases have come and gone.
Though we have missed you dear,
In candles' glow we see your love,
And know that you are here.

To Johnny

Given to him on the day of his marriage

If all the things I wished for you
Could be revealed and then come true,
You'd be just rich enough to know
That some things last but riches go.
That there are poor folks everywhere
Who need your help to fight despair;
You'd be just strong enough to say
A "no" to many things some day;
You'd be just smart enough to learn
That those who play with fire will burn;
You'd know there was a God, my dear,
It was His love that brought you here.
You'd find the girl to be your wife
Who'd walk beside you down through life
And love you through the good and bad
And share your dreams with you, my lad;
But if these be denied to you
I'd wish a faith to see you through-
A faith so strong that you will pray
All these things for your child someday.

"I wrote this shortly after you were born. I've been waiting for the "right" time to give it to you. Today is the day!! Bless you both—Mom"

Sleepy Child

Sleepy child with eyes of blue
You have a fortune little lad
You own this house and more than that
You've captivated Mom and Dad.

While people wait to do your will
You lie and gurgle at the wall
You're king of this, your world, my boy,
You have no worries, child, at all.

You have the nicest baby way
Of splattering food, of throwing things:
Your manners somehow hardly are
The ones we would expect in kings.

Be very happy, little man
For kinghood passes, you are blessed
With baby joys, so close your eyes
And pleasant dreams while you're at rest.

To Lynn Upon Her Marriage To Chris

May 24, 2007

Lynnie, how we've loved you
From the moment of your birth
When a winsome little creature
That cried, and sighed and burped,
Took her little fingers, held on tightly
Refusing to let go.
Oh, we loved you so.

We watched you grow
Like a flower opening petals,
Reaching out to see what's there,
And finding, I surmises—
Surprises.
Frustrations, new relations, with books, schools and friends
And all the many things that "growing up" sends.

We want the life that lies ahead for you
To be a glorious time with sorrows few,
Full of many splendid things
That life devises.
Lots of hugs and lots of Lynn's tinkling laughter
And, oh yes, lots of kisses ever after
And always to know
How we love you so

Peter—A Grand Child

When Peter comes a' calling we just have the greatest fun,
We look in every cranny and we're always on the run.
The toy box is open, its temptations all abound,
But Peter seems enchanted by other things around.
No treasures from the toy box, he wants the crystal vase,
The place he loves the very best is in the fireplace.

Peter is athletic; he creeps down all the halls
At eighty miles an hour, and he does this without pause.
He loves the toilet paper and I think that on the whole
He likes it even better than he likes the toilet bowl.

The dogs are very wary when Peter comes to stay;
They are not overjoyed at all, they slowly slink away
Returning only when he eats. For Peter food is great,
But more of it goes on the floor than stays upon his plate.

He smells of peanut butter, there are crackers every place;
His hair is filled with jam and there is egg upon his face,
So Peter has a bath and how he chortles full of glee
While eating soap and splashing sudsy bubbles over me.

He makes me think he's tired as he yawns upon my lap;
With great anticipation I put him down to nap.
No luck! The yawn was boredom. Does this come as any news?
Peter really wanted in the closet with the shoes.

Peter takes command of all; the house is really his.
Peter isn't perfect—but his Grammie thinks he is!

Peter's Graduation

Is this the boy who loved to crawl
As fast as he could down the length of the hall?
Who only stopped by the bathroom door
For the toilet paper that he loved more
Than just about anything. He would sit
In the fireplace gleefully unrolling it.

Is this the boy who could reach the sky
On his skateboard? Wow! Is this the guy?
Ready to go this happy day
Into the world to make his way?
That little boy with a grin on his face
Will make this world just a wonderful place.

Gems

This was read at the marriage in Brazil of Jonathan Paine to Rosie.

Some of us go for amethysts
We're wild for their lovely hue
While others of us are the emerald type
And don't really care for blue.

And the depth of the color of rubies
Makes some of us start to drool;
The aquamarines just are splendid
The opals are really "cool."

We "oohed" and we "ahed" at their beauty
And questioned and touched at will,
And each of us thought we had purchased
The prettiest stone in Brazil.

But one thing we all are agreed on
Unanimously I recall:
Jonathan, you are getting
The loveliest gem of all.

Rosie!

To Aunt Ruth

September 28, 1985

We went to say "goodbye" to you—
We held your hand in ours and there
We felt the vigor of your life,
The need to be and do and care.

We looked deep in your eyes and saw
Profundity of perfect blue,
But you were looking far beyond
To other realms—you knew, you knew.

We kissed your cheek and lingered still
Bathed in a love that families show
Each to the other—comforting—
When some must stay and some must go.

We said "goodbye" but not farewell
For you are with us as before,
And we will hold your hand again
Someday—somewhere—we're sure, we're sure.

What Mother Means

Dedicated to my mother, Loretta J. Bell

I try to find the words which tell the world
How much my mother means to me today-
There are no words, there is no way that I
May speak of her nor even start to say
The wondrous things she taught me as a child-
How can you tell of love, of faith so rare
That suddenly when you were grown you found
Your mother in her way had placed it there?
How can you speak of joy when joy just was
childhood—a radiant shiny time
Which reaches now into your very life
And still makes living seem a thing sublime?
How can you tell of wisdom when you know
In looking back that schools could never teach
Rare insight into God and trials of man?
My mother gave to me a touch of each.
And somehow quietly she walked a path
She knew I'd follow on my own someday.
How blessed I was that she with patient care
Did not point me very far astray.
And I thank God what she revealed to me—
Mothers are not born with courage strong
Nor faith, nor hope for children yet to be,
Nor wisdom to determine right from wrong;
For women are born, but mothers come to be
Only by hard work and many tears
And ceaseless vigil o'er the things once held dear
Which never ever wavers through the years.
I guess this was the greatest thing she taught
For when I think I've failed it always seems
I hear her saying, "Don't despair, work on,"
For this is what being "Mother" means.

A Mother's Prayer

Dear Lord, I have been blessed by oh so much;
A golden childhood, filled with all the things
That childhood needs-abounding joy and love,
Security-the steadiness it brings.

And faith instilled by parents who have known
How much a child will need his faith in life
How often will that faith be called upon
In deepest sorrow, times of darkest strife.

I, who count so many blessings, pray
For wisdom now that I too may lead
As I was led, by those with insight rare
Who trained their children first by word and deed.

I do not ask for all the answers, Lord,
I know my questions are age-old to you.
I pray just as my mother must have prayed
For guidance and for answers to a few.

What Is A Mother

A changer of diapers
A stopper of wails
A hand holder, face wiper
Hearer of tales.
A good tucker-inner,
A cleaner of ears,
A judge and a jury,
A drier of tears.
A reader of literature
"Baby bear said—"
And a listener to lecturers
"Is your child well-fed?"
A taxi cab driver,
A fixer of things,
A builder of sandcastles
(Homes of kings),
A fervent believer
In power of prayer,
A molder of angels
With insight rare.
A determined being
To pave the way
For better things
And a better day.

To Mother

One of many birthday poems to her. She kept them all in her cedar chest.

It has been my observation
As the years fly swiftly thro
That to wish a happy birthday
And no more will never do.
But to add my fondest wishes
That those things you hold so dear,
The dreams you've had and all your hopes
Will just come true this year.
Is also not the answer
For sometimes 'tis sad indeed
The things we want the most in life
Are not the things we need.
And so I think I'll send this wish—
The nicest I could find—
May all the things you wish for
Be the things God has in mind.

On Mother's Day

You cannot "air mail" love
Nor can you send
Those fleeting thoughts that came to you
At odd times through the hurried days and weeks,
Just little thoughts of what you say or do

You cannot package up with frilly bows
Things closest to your heart,
But you can pray
That all the words unsaid
          the love, respect
Will still be felt
Though you be miles away

And so with hopes that you will understand
This wish of mine—Though certainly not new—
May Mothers Day be happy and so filled with love
Enough to make a joyful year
For you.

To Mother On Her Birthday

If I could bear my wishes home
Upon a breath of Spring
I'd wish you all the happiness
That this fine day could bring-
I'd wish for joys abundant
For gladness everywhere
And most of all you'd know I want
Just to be there.
And when I close my eyes to think
Of you as you are,
Somehow the miles are shortened
And you don't seem so far.
So may the day be happy
Full of joy in all you do,
And may you feel a little more
My great love for you.

Treasures For Mother

What treasure should I bring to share with you?
If only I'd been blessed with just a few
T'would be no problem if I only had
A small amount of things for which I'm glad.
I treasure things like sounds of rain at night
Or moonshine on the snow so clear and bright;
A favorite poem my mother read to me,
A fog horn's haunting roll across the sea,
A quilt with patches of a dress I wore,
My Raggedy Ann whose face my puppy tore.
A photo album filled with memories kind
Of treasured days of those now left behind,
A Valentine home made with labored care.
A locket with a bit of baby hair—
But I must say that treasured most by me
Is God's best gift and that is memory.

To My Mother

Upon entering Chapter Eternal March 1, 1980

My mother would have loved to see
The brilliant array
Which blossomed in the winter cold
In Iowa that day.

My mother would have loved to walk
That garden path and know
That God, as He is prone to do,
Brings flowers in the snow.

But she and He were talking
Of another garden spot.
Of fertilizing, mulching,
What would grow and what would not.

Forgotten were the things on earth
For she had happily met
A Gardener who said that in heaven
She could grow the violet.

(President of the Iowa African Violet Society)

Iowa Youth

My brother Howard, Mother, Yours Truly, Dad

Air Castles

Very first poem written—age 8

I'll build a castle in the sky
A product of my dreams
It is not made of rustic bricks
But mine is one that gleams.

The roof will be all patched with stars
The moon will make it gay
The land the King and Queen walk down
Will be the Milky Way.

Its towers will be filled with gold
This to the poor I'll give
And then when I grow very old
I'll go up there to live.

Mourning Dove

Spring in Iowa—1937

Mournful though your cry may be
We have been waiting long,
Through the blasts of wintertime
Just to hear your song.

Forlornly perched upon a twig
You pour forth melody
Though white may be the earth below
And gray each ghostly tree.

The world around may be disturbed
By your song, early bird,
But you are welcome, for you are
The first of spring we've heard.

A High Schooler's Thoughts

I haven't seen all of this country of mine
But before the long passage of time
I hope to see all of it—hamlets and lanes
Waterfalls, mountains, oceans and plains
I have no desire to see London or France
I just would like to be given the chance
To travel America, to see and know
The great surging whole of it, before I go.
But wherever I'd travel
What e'er I would do
I'm sure I would always feel this true.
The impressionable years—the
Years that seemed best
Were spent on the lap of the middle west.

US—*1940*

We're seventeen
Inclined to blush
We know it all
Which isn't much.

We like flat shoes
Our hair in curls
Adore soft sweaters
And scads of pearls.

We like the fellows
We think they're swell
Most of them, Who?
We can't tell.

But off the record
We might say
The ones that have
That certain way.

To sip a Coke
Is superfine
We'll take a Coke
Most anytime.

And formal dances
The deluxe way
Oh, how we like to
Swing and sway.

And we know this
Will raise a fuss,
But we can't find
Much wrong with us!

Home

Written in high school in Iowa

No mansion with its pillars towering high
Can ever be
A home to me,
For when the sun creeps out across the sky
And birds so gay
Chirp through the day,
And morning glories twine about the door
In heavenly shade, then I can ask no more.

Let other men have palaces and towers
And spacious gardens filled with growing flowers
And tall fir trees.
Just give me a plot of rich, black loam
And I, with aid from rain and sun,
Will make it home.

Country Lanes

I like the twisting country lanes
The air is fresh, the earth is dark
And everywhere are living things
A small gray squirrel, a meadowlark.

And all are friendly little folk
They talk you over, stare awhile
And then they scamper off to play.
I never watch but what I smile.

If all the world were just a lane,
A friendly lane where folk at play
Would only turn and stare at you
If you, by chance, would come their way.

Country Church

Situated near Mt. Hammil, Iowa
where my father worshipped as a boy

If I could paint a little Iowa town
Or choose from country sides some peaceful scene
I know I would include a tiny church
With whitewashed walls and churchyard calm-serene.

The faith within is precious and more rare
Than artificial work of time
The quiet hope, sincere belief in God
Is something sacred, very near divine.

No grand and glorious stain-glassed windows there
Each window, doorway, frames the Maker's art
Their altar, simply hewn from native pine
And silent prayers are felt deep in each heart.

The neat trim churchyard-monument to those
Who used to worship there and now are gone
Remains, and honored dead sleep peacefully
Beneath a lilac bush, a rose, an Iowa dawn.

If God who once looked down and called it good
Is doubtful now, with war and crime and dearth,
May He behold this church, its faithful folk—
A tiny spot of heaven on his earth.

Pearl Harbor

Written in high school

They laid the goal that grim December morn
When souls were warped and human bodies torn,
Their planes of death blazed paths across the sky
For us to follow, to return or die.

Their mocking laughter far across the sea
Half crazed our minds—we who were always free.
We asked no questions, turned toward the West
And grimly set about upon our quest.

We knew there would be blood and sweat and tears
We've learned that lesson well down through the years
For bombs of death that fell from skies of gray
Have set our course, and we'll avenge that day.

Attention—1942

High school thoughts

Eyes straight
Shoulders high
Left right
Marching by,

Bugle call
Cuts the air,
Drums roll
Everywhere

Uniforms
Starched and clean
Gold buttons
Glow and gleam.

Soldiers marching off today
To fight in lands far away?
The High School band
Eyes straight ahead
At a football game
Drilling—instead.

The University Of Iowa

Words and music sung in University of Iowa contest 1945—
Alpha Delta Pi—FIRST PLACE!

A river flowing onward
That bears our namesake true
A dome where glorious sunsets
Have cast a golden hue.

The rolling hills
With soft, green grass
And stately old oak trees,
In years to come with gladness,
We'll think on all of these.

The corridors of learning,
The halls familiar yet,
The friendships formed forever
All these we won't forget.

As long as leaves turn in the fall
And place old gold on high,
As long as our old Capitol
Points ever to the sky

Then loyal sons of Iowa,
Each daughter proud and true,
Will stand with overflowing heart,
Beside you—Iowa U.

My Heart

Written on Thanksgiving—my first in Florida

My heart has found the long way home today
Across the plains it has come to rest
Beneath the stately oaks and maples
It knows best.

And it has paused awhile within those walls
Each board familiar, each familiar face
And given thanks with them
In its old place.

For though, like many
I have had to roam
I am not lonely now—
My heart is home.

You Can Go Home Again

Written for 50 year H.S. reunion—Colfax, Iowa

From urban sprawls and
        beaches by the sea
        From mountains, hazy blue
        Or wild and free
        You can go home.

And you can live once more
        Fond memories kind when
        we were all so clever
        and "old"—a word—
        and fifty years—forever!
But you can live once more.

And you can share again
        Fall nights—full of football
        Full of fun
        Of orange and black
        a high school band
        High stepping in the sun.
These you can share.

And pictures of the past can
        show again
        In merciful memory
        classmates gone from us;
        The pleasures of a
        thousand wild good times
        Delightfully discussed
For pictures bring them back.

You can go home again
    Reliving shining times
    and years that seemed the best
    Happily, blissfully, safely
    spent in the middle west
It's good to be home again.

Nature

George and I at the start of the Mississippi

Rain In Spring
Written when in High School

Rain in spring does funny things
Sometimes it falls in vicious drops
Life stops
To watch it come,
But glorious colors spring rain brings.
Sometimes it is a feathery rain
Our lane
Is barely dampened,
But earth is warm and my heart sings.

Jenny Wren's Spring Talk

I overheard you weeks ago
      Chattering in a tree;
Saw you cock your little head
      Maliciously at me.

You looked in every cranny,
      Left unturned no stone
And contemptuously regarded
      Any newly painted home.

You passed right by the sign which read:
      "For rent just for a song",
And you settled in a well-worn house
      To live the summer long.

You scoured your house from roof to perch
      Sat in a near-by tree
And scolded any neighbor
      Who dropped by there just for tea.

And you've worried and you've fretted
      Acted at your worst;
You've almost driven us away.
      You know-we lived here first!

Now you think you have a secret
      Just as dark as it can be,
But I heard your babies, Jenny,
      And I had a peek to see!

Hope

I plant the seeds with hope that they will grow,
With care their special placement I apprise,
That they will come along I do not know.

I till and mulch the gravid earth just so
Then God and I together supervise:
I plant the seeds with hope that they will grow.

The golden sunshine sheds its rays below;
Before the rain I try to fertilize
If I have timed it right I do not know.

I plant the seeds with hope that they will grow.
To plan too far ahead is never wise,
Sometimes it seems they come along so slow—

The weeks go by, it seems so long ago
I look for them with undespairing eyes;
I plant the seeds with hope that they will grow.

'Tis so with life;
You really never know.
You only hope and sometimes rationalize,
You do your best and hope it will be so.
You plant the seeds with hope that they will grow.

Sea Turtle

She came ashore from out a placid sea-
    A gutted moon revealed her panoply-
        Her need was there; she moved laboriously.
Displacing sand in furrows, on she crept,
    Grotesque her horny skull, grotesque except
        Her patient eyes, her gentle eyes that wept.
Her ponderous bulk inched slowly to a space
    Above the tide. She hollowed out a place
        To steadfastly begin (or end) her race.
The massive creature slipped into the sand
    Mother-soft her seed. With flipper hand
        She gently covered them—trusting—and
Regretfully, she turned—with misted sight
    Following an age-old solemn rite
        Painfully, she slid into the night.

Land Use

The land lay-vastly content, secure
    with a discernable awareness,
    its limpid pools regarding the creatures
    who called it home.

Wrapped in a blanket of quiescense,
    Lulled by the dulcet dialogue of song birds,
    Complacent with diurnal matters,
    Replete with knowledge of summer, autumn, winter and spring.
        Isn't eternity forever?

Came the Executioner one dawn-
    A cataclysmic cacophony of bull-jaws, dozer-demolition
    Consuming, shattering, devastating-

Fall Comes To North Carolina

As the dawn arrives
The air is chill;
There's dew upon the lawn,
And birds sing quietly
Of summer—gone.

So still a thing—this summer going into fall,
Not colorful—not gay—
Not frantic in its will to last.
But topped by azure skies, a hot, still noon
Remains alone of summer—past.

Friendship

"The Gluttons"
Very close friends

It's In The Bag

To a friend upon leaving for a trip to Great Britain

The art of the cook is exploited
In thousands and thousands of ways,
But anyone who has traveled
Will tout with grandiose praise

Some cheese on the banks of the Avon
Along with some wine of course,
As Shakespeare has said "That's rapture!"
It takes away any remorse!

And the moors in the North of Scotland
Seem to take on a glow that's divine
Whenever the fare is bread and cheese-
Along with a little wine!

And County Clare is greener
When you see it through misty rain
After having a repast with vino
In a little Irish lane.

So whether you lunch in a ruin
Or 'neath thatch that's beginning to sag,
The success of your trip is unquestioned—
It's literally "In the bag!"

Good Friends Traveling— To Marilyn And Slats

March 2, 1996

We've seen the wild beauty of Yorkshire
And the wind off the moors we've felt.
We've watched as a glorious rainbow
Vaulted the land of the Celt.

We've gazed on the Alps in their splendor,
Relaxed in the gardens of Kew,
Raised many a glass in our travels,
And "raised me Tommy" too!

We've B and B'd in the country,
Rejoiced at a lilac bouquet,
Traveled the length of Britain,
And "raspberried" all the way!

We've sailed to the Grecian islands,
In the emerald Aegean Sea,
Climbed the Acropolis hillside—
Oh, we've seen so much, you and we.

Through the years we have laughed together
And cried every now and then,
But oh, the years have been golden,
And wouldn't we do it again?

Ode To Neighbors

For Peter and Anne

There are some neighbors who measure their lot lines
And step off with care every inch
And neighbors who can't stand the wild life
And would like every rabbit to lynch.

And some neighbors who peek through their windows
And spy on the things that you do,
And neighbors who seem to take pleasure
To criticize, even to sue.

However—

There are neighbors who leap to the rescue
When squirrels grow corn on your site—
Neighbors who phone for instructions
When things at your place don't seem right.

And neighbors who meet in their bathrobes
On the porch in the early light
And decide great issues of merit
Like just what tree would be right.

So—

These neighbors deserve recognition,
A medal or even a star.
They live next door and we thank them
For being the folks that they are!

Sisters

Written for my sister P.E.O.'s

I never had a sister as I grew.
The joys that sisters share I never knew;
But now I have a million sisters dear
And all the joys of sisterhood are clear.

I feel the caring that my sisters show
When skies aren't always blue, and clouds hang low.
For through the valley they will walk with me
And with the Lord will hold my hand, you see.

And graciously they'll listen as I talk
Of mundane things and sometimes when I sulk!
And they will let me "get it off my chest"
And nod most knowingly when that seems best.

And they are kind when I'm inclined to state
How much I know; they just "kindly" wait!
Yet they will speak out when they feel they must
Defending something treasured, something just.

My happy sisters laugh a lot and sing
And to the world a certain joy they bring.
Blessed am I; the love my sisters share
Speaks from the heart and shows how much they care

To Slats

Written upon the death of a dear friend

Have a great time, Slats, you and George,
You've so much to talk about, things you've shared:
Camping together in rain or shine,
Building a campfire that was fine,
Singing out lustily in the choir,
You can sing now, fellows, (only higher).
And traveling abroad with a car that was leased
The laughter and joking never ceased!
You dined on the Avon—if you please—
With Shakespeare and your wine and cheese,
And you wanted the car to have a wash!
Well, George disagreed with that of course,
On a Scottish moor or a Grecian isle
Each day was ended with a smile.
We'll miss you, Slats, but we want you to know
That a lot of folks waiting here below
See you and George smiling in such a way
That we know all is well and you're okay.

Memorial To Paul Wolfe

Who always climbed the ridges

Oh I have walked my way on mountain trails,
Climbed the rocky parapets to the sky;
I've seen the eminence of the ponderous peaks
Hushed and silent, standing heaven-high.

And I have made my bed beneath the stars
In scintillating splendor over me;
I've hiked where rainbowed rivers race
In frothing fury downward to the sea.

And I have felt the rush of wind up there
Its savage strength-gleeful in its might;
Seen the sun rise on a snowy plain,
Aurora gold disseminating light.

Oh it was good-to walk the ridges there,
To gaze into the vast empyreal blue;
To catch a glimpse of heaven's peace, I think
Is granted only to a very few.

Teaching

A Happy Teacher

A Teacher Speaks

Neatly precisive,
Staring at you
Green eyes and brownish,
Grey-tinged and blue-
Brightly alert eyes
Seeking to know,
Quietly questioning,
Hoping to know.

Eyes that stare blankly
Unable to grasp,
Pulled down by a culture,
Held back by the past.
Eyes full of laughter,
Doe eyes, lashes curled;
Drug clouded eyes
That have turned off the world.

Each morning I ask
The Lord for a way
To light up those eyes
This day.

An English Teacher's Lament

As authorities clamor
To stop teaching grammar
I can't help but chortle with glee.
Who, whom and whoever
Have certainly never
Been known as my cup of tea.

So I read how to clear up
Grammatical "smear up"—
"Paint out their mistakes as they write!"
And armed with red pencil
(*That* seemed most essential)
I went forth to do the good fight.

And I must say never
Have I ever, ever
Seen verbals used so many ways.
Participles that dangle
And mix in the tangle
Of each prepositional phrase.

And talk about tenses
T'was utterly senseless
To try to explain about past,
When nobody knew
What a verb had to do
Or a period belonged at the last.

So when all of my classes
Had red marks in masses
I quietly counted to ten,
And after reflection
With strong interjection
We're now back at grammar again!

Thoughts Of An English Teacher

Our names might not be found on any lists
Of twentieth century poets, I fear.
No school child will recall a line of ours
Nor hold some couplet we have done, as dear.
Our names may never grace the sacred shelves
Of musty archives found across the land;
Posterity may never be aware
Of tercits we have penned, nor understand
That we have looked at dawn and seen new hope,
Have peered beyond the first soft light of day,
Have watched a ship upon a mirrored sea
And written of life and places far away.
So be it! You and I have touched a flower
And seen the promise that a rainbow brings,
Have known lackluster days of wintertime
And found in shrouded mists, some golden Springs.
Perhaps our quatrains that we file away
Some relative in ages hence will read
Exclaiming, "Why! They're good!" They'll only voice
What we knew all the time. Are you agreed?

School Days

Each fall when school bells ring across our land
Proud parents take their children by the hand
And walk with them to school doors open wide;
With mixed emotions each will go inside.
Some are terrified, will shy away,
Others smile and gaily plan to stay,
And some will never show us how they feel
But will keep silent and will not reveal
Some spite that comes to them—or unkind word,
A hurried teacher's chance remark—but heard!
And we, as parents, who with faith have sent
A child to school know "as the twig is bent"—
We now must watch that they grow straight and tall
Must guard their rights—must see that they learn all
Must make the schools, the teachers, well aware
That we are not indifferent—that we care.
For school doors open wide this first full day
Must not be closed to us in any way;
And we, though human, must be akin
To God and strive through faith to win
Our child's full confidence that he will share
With us these years of growing up a treasure rare;
And shared experience will come to be
Mile posts in our own maturity.

My Church

Celtic Cross atop Lakeside Presbyterian Church

On Building An Addition For My Church

Dear Lord accept our humble thanks
For You have walked with us
Through some stormy days
And the mountainous maze
Of plans for an edifice.

And each brick and stone which was put in place
Was really laid there by You,
For You were the builder
Of plans that bewilder
And we were merely the crew.
So, Lord, please accept our gratitude
For all of your loving aid,
And help us to know
That wherever we go
We're still crew of your crusade.
The Church is much more than a building
More than the folks inside;
It stands in its glory
To help spread your story
To everyone—to all—worldwide.

My Church
Lakeside Presbyterian

My Church means 1000 things to me—
      caring and sharing
      dying and crying,
      birthing and mirthing,
a cushion for adversity,
a catapult for celebration.

My Church means one Celtic cross pointed high
      in Presbyterian correctness,
      silent quintessence,
      the very essence
of my belief.

My Church means a window looking East
      in prismatic perfection
      a joyous convection
      a silent reflection
of the face of God.

My Church means
      fellowship—mellowship
      and certainly "hello" ship
      and meeting and eating
      and joyously greeting—
a melding of 1000 occasions.

My Church means the unreserved laughter of children
      candidly wanting to know,
      faces alive with a glow,
      voices resounding in glee
      singing to God and to you and to me.

My Church does mean 1000 things to me
      but most of all is the love of one another,
      the unqualified caring for each other—

      Built on land
      That is sand
      But rock solid.

That's what my Church is to me.

Thoughts From An Elder
In Lakeside Presbyterian Church

Dear God we thank you that we may
In silence bow our heads today,
For all good things along our way-
For friendships strong which you have blessed,
For strength to rise from pettiness,
For courage to withstand each test;
For thoughts not said, for deeds not won
Give us the strength at set of sun
To go ahead with things undone.
In all we do, in all we say
Show us God, the proper way
But teach us first to kneel and pray
Thy will be done.

For Lakeside Presbyterian Church Choir

I've sung in lots of choirs and I know
The special glow
Of a mute pianissimo
Of a thunderous fortissimo
And I have thought that maybe, just maybe,
These notes were a start
Of what was in my heart
Of what I longed to share,

Giving from the soul
Is a role for those who sing;

And now because God has His plan
I sit enthralled, listening,
And am taken by our choir
Just a little higher then I am,
Away from menial tasks,
Out of media blasts,
Shielded from political impasse,

THANK YOU, CHOIR

Ode To Harold Bradley

To our choir director from his "birds who fly north in the summer—

Here's a "hello" from the gang up north.
It's tempted us, Harold, to sally forth
To be with you on this day of days
'Cause you've meant so much in so many ways.
We who can hardly warble at all
You've pulled together and we have a ball!
And how many times we've heard it said,
"I won't wait if you don't go ahead!"
And we've learned the life of Robert Shaw,
His ways of teaching—we know them all!
Our "Hallelujahs" aren't always right
And you worked on our "*ah*mens" many a night,
And you've warned us, Harold, to please not sound
Like just any choir from someplace around!!
"Spit out your consonants", you would say
"If you spray your neighbor, that's OKAY!"
And "Sing some note even if it's wrong"
And "Smile like an angel full of song!"
We love you, Harold, and this is *so* true
Thank you, thank you, for just being you.

Holidays

Santa (George) and Me

Thoughts At Easter

Mary was a mother
And Mary bowed her head,
She sang a simple lullabye
Beside a baby's bed.

She kissed his hurts and fed Him
And taught him all she knew.
She planted in his heart her love
And, like the Child, it grew.

She washed his grubby fingers,
Taught Him how to find
The path of righteousness and then
She gave Him to mankind.

And after all the glory,
And after all the tears,
Mary thought in silence
Of the long, lost years.

For Mary was His mother
And a bit of her must die
Each time we turn away from Him
And once more—Crucify.

Thanksgiving Day

(Remember when this was a "problem" for our government?)

The question before our nation isn't
A matter of drought or of fire
Or whether to give up everything
And at sixty-five retire.

It isn't a question of war or peace
Or of preserving the nation's trees,
But what we're all wondering about
Is when to cook our turkeys.

If the pilgrims ever heard of this
They'd shake their heads and say,
"For goodness sakes who thought of this
And why so much trouble anyway?"

"We didn't dream we'd cause a row,
We were thankful we were living.
We don't care what day you use
Make every day Thanksgiving!"

Prayer At Thanksgiving—1998

Dear Lord, I drove across the Iowa plains
And saw the mammoth piles of golden grains
Rotting and wasted, and I wonder why
When all across your world the hungry die.

And nightly T. V.'s strident blaring sound
Recites a thousand horrors all around-
An earthquake, fire, a bomb, a missing child-
Abuse and hate and fear—a world defiled.

Dear Lord, I am a woman and I know
Experiencing some pain will help me grow;
But I would ask your help—I am so blessed—
Please point the way that I may help the rest.

Thoughts This Thanksgiving

If for just a moment's time we'd stop today
And think of those who went ahead and forged their way
Through terrors just as great to them as nuclear war,
Through pestilence and famine, and even more
The fear of the unknown—for just as we
They did not know what lay ahead; they could not see.
And all of those that rode the wagon trails,
The sturdy ones that laid the golden rails
Could never know if they would live or die,
But they had faith, were brave, and they would try!
For those brave forbears of ours who stopped and prayed
To God, at Harvest times, were not afraid,
And they begat a nation proud and free
A sacred trust passed on to you and me.
And as you think, remember this today
This country did not come to men who ran away;
It was not made by men who would not speak;
Nor was it built by those who would not seek!
It might be well, in all our haste, that we
Would pause and pray for their integrity.

Thanksgiving

If we can't be thankful at all today
For anything that has come our way
If we've searched our hearts and still can't find
A single thing for a little prayer
Then we haven't watched the shining sand
And held on tight to a grimy hand
Or rocked a child to sleep at night
And he was afraid and we held him tight.
Then we haven't seen the morning sun
And felt the miracle of day begun
And we haven't heard our children cry
When they were hurt and we asked God why?
I think we've a prayer Thanksgiving Day
We've all so much we ought to say.

First Christmas

Written at age 11

A shepherd came to Bethlehem
To walk its lowly streets
And looked inside the stable door
And saw the Savior fast asleep.

He asked if there was any room
For him to lay his head
In a place nearby the stable door
Where holy feet had tread.

When told there was no such a room
He slowly turned away
And wondered if he too like the Child
Could rest upon the hay.

He opened up the stable door
And with eyes so blue and mild
Asked if He could rest awhile
Beside the sleeping Child.

He could not sleep from one lone star
Which lit the room with light
And he wondered why this stable
Seemed draped in holy light.

And he wondered why men came
And offered a small prayer
Beside the sleeping Child's bed
In the stillness of night air.

We today are that shepherd
And in every Christmas home
We reenact the story
That the stars to mankind show,

But we know that one lone shepherd taught
That that Child of lowly birth
That he gazed at with wondering eyes
Was God's son come to Earth.

Thoughts 1963

I've just returned from Christmas land,
At least it seemed that way,
For the snow fell silently and hid
The scars of yesterday.
And the bare trees donned their sparkling gowns
Resplendent for a ball—
My heart returned to my childhood
When this didn't seem strange at all.
And wise men trudging through the drifts
Of heavy winter snow
Toward a baby warmly wrapped
Against the winds that blow
Didn't seems out of place to me—
For my childhood was that way
And all the joys of that far away time
Came back to me that day.
But now transported by modern wings
To palm tree land again
I see the wise men walking
Through sand to Bethlehem
And I catch the shine of the candles
And the glow of the Christmas tree
And I realize that Christmas
Is a state of mind, you see.

Whether Christmas in the Northland
Or Christmas way back when,
Or Christmas right here at home
It all comes back to men.
If men so live their lives to show
For people everywhere
A warm and loving feeling—
That they really care—
That that which hurts another
Is painful too for all;
That when another's crying
All men should heed the call
For love is what makes Christmas
Not snow or tinsely arts,
For men are keeping Christmas
If love is in the heart.

On That First Christmas Morn

There wasn't any frenzy
Of people-somewhat wild!
But wise men plodded onward
Searching for the Child.

And shepherds on the hilltops
Heard choirs from above
Sing the Christmas message
Of peace, and hope, and love.

Once there was a Christmas
When a star shone dazzling bright,
And guided gentle folk around
To Him, on Christmas night.

Oh, I must hurry home from town
Where tinsely Christmas trees
Beckon from each window
To gifts "just sure to please!"

And I must open wide my door
And let the Christ Child in,
That we may have a Christmas
In His honor, once again.

I'd Like To Go To Bethlehem Again

I'd like to go to Bethlehem
I long to see once more
Where wise men saw the stable
With the straw strewn floor.
I yearn to see the radiance
And the glow in Mary's eyes
When Joseph smiled in greeting
To those men so wise.
I want to see where shepherds
With their sheep close by
Heard the angels' tidings
Out there beneath the sky.
I yearn to witness miracles
Like that Baby's birth.
I hunger for the kind of love
His coming brought the earth.
But I am here a world away
From Bethlehem and still
Could miracles be wrought by men
Of monumental will?
Oh, I pray that there will come
A path for all of them
That leads to unrequited love
And another Bethlehem.

A Christmas Card For Today

Dear Lord, walk with us as we go
About our tasks this Christmas time;
Let us not miss the story told
By every carol, every chime.

Bear with us as we seem somehow
To minimize the Savior's birth;
Priorities are sometimes wrong
'Midst all this revelry and mirth.

A little Baby soon gets lost
Beneath the tinsel bright and gay;
It seems that we must learn again
The meaning of this sacred day.

Oh God, we ask that you will be
Our Guide, and walk with us again,
Along the dusty winding road
That leads once more to Bethlehem.

Christmas Memories

The littlest angel is tucked in bed,
The Night Before Christmas" has just been read,
The stockings are hung by the chimney with care
And Santa Claus sits and relaxes there.
The tree lights twinkle a friendly glow,
The hi-fi is playing, but very low.
This is the time that will always bring
The quiet peace of remembering
Other Christmases long ago
When the house grew still and the fires burned low;
Childhood laughter and tinsel bright,
Faces aglow with the Christmas light;
The welcome snow at Christmastide,
The bitter wind, but the warmth inside;
The arrival of Santa in his sleigh
On a downtown street of a Saturday
Melodious chimes from the church's spire,
The not-so-melodious cherub choir.
And drifting back from the days of yore
I wish, as my mother did before,
In the bayberry candle's final glow;
I wish and it will come true I know.
Oh, I'd love to wrap in a package gay
So the children could find it on Christmas day
Tucked in under our Christmas tree
The wonderful gift of memory.

Oh! Christmas Tree!

The yearly decision has come for us.
We treat it with proper pomp and fuss.
We sally forth each with thought in mind
Of the sort of tree we're going to find.
Should it be this one, or should it be that?
Should it be sleek, or should it be fat?
Does it have character? How on a lot
Can a tree have character in that spot?

When we've struggled through every "if" "but" or "maybe,"
We carry it home like a new born baby,
And treat it with deference fit for a queen,
And declare it's the very best one we've seen.

It's placed in a stand and it mustn't teeter,
And it's straight, not leaning one millimeter,
And its best side becomes a terrible issue,
We turn and we turn. Oh, I just wish you
Could see the problems of nestling down
The loveliest Christmas tree in town.

But the last light's working; the tinsel is there,
Each ornament's placed with loving care,
The star is glowing for all to see;
And who's the wearier—us or the tree?

I'm Waiting For The Muse

I was waiting on the muse
    I was waiting on the muse
    of poetry—that is!
And you know how 'tis
    with muses!!
They comes when they chooses!!

So at 2 o'clock A.M.
(and I don't do mornings!)
    Muse awakened me and then
        He said, "I should remember
        Since we are finally in December
It's NOW okay to think of Christmas
    and all that jazz and razz ma taz!"

"But when you're Christmas shopping
Checking lists until you're dropping
You should not forget the Baby
(Hope He's on your list) and maybe
    You could give some gifts to Him:

    More love for weary workers,
    Strong faith for church's shirkers,
    True justice for our courts of law,
    Hope for the future in the minds of all;"

Muse said, "No sleep for you
    at two or three of four or evermore
Until you work out this peace thing
    for that Baby—and maybe
For yourselves."

Thoughts At New Year's Eve

Year's end invariably brings to us all
A review of the days and a brief recall
Of the months just past with heartaches and pain—
Sunshine and gladness, shadows and rain.

And the years stretch back
From the now to the then,
And we even see things
As they might have been.

We see some corners we wouldn't turn
If we went again, and yes, we learn
That though some of the roads were dark as night
Where we groped our way for there was no light,
In retrospect we are able to say
We're better because we went that way.

For memories invariably help us see
That God has known better the way then we;
Looking back shows we had nothing to dread
And bestows a courage to look ahead.

In Conclusion

"It's A Wonderful Life"

Grief's Slow Wisdom

At first I had a grief so hard to bear,
A pain so deep it seemed beyond repair
And with the pain my mind, laboriously slow,
Refused to think—refused to see and know.

Except it could not cope with dreams that came,
In sleep when life went on still just the same.
And when I thought that I could not endure,
God's voice came gentle, firm and sure,

"Reach out your hand to me in faith," He said,
"And then go on, fear not the days ahead."
The weeks went by, the heart survived some way,
The ache seemed less with every passing day.

My mind grew well and able now at last,
To picture with less pain the recent past,
For I had come to know that grief you see
Is certain love and part of me.

One Day To Live

January 20, 1960

If I had just one day in which to live
What would I do—how would I pass each hour?
I think I would arise at dawn to see once more
God's glory painted there and power.

I would not criticize all that last day
But loved ones, held close, would be heard—
We'd talk, just daily talk, and laugh and love
And I would savor every precious word.

I know I would take time to pay a call
On someone sick, or someone feeling low;
While sands of time ran out I'd try to cheer
An aching heart—(I'd meant to, long ago).

I'd walk beside the sea; I'd feel the wind—
I'd hold a rose within my hand and touch
The velvet petals—beauty in a world
Where beauty can be seen in oh so much!

And at day's end, as each star twinkled on,
I'd watch the miracle of night,
No different than before,
It only then began to mean much more.

If I had just one day in which to live
At that day's close I would review the past—
I'm sure my only wish would be that I'd made time
To live all days as I had lived the last.

A Prayer

Dear Lord,
    I pray that I may never cease to feel
            Sublimely stirred when I behold a rose
            In petal-perfect beauty,
            Velvet soft,
            Auroral dew
            Enveloping its repose;
    That I may never fail to hear
            The strength,
            Endlessly enduring
            As the sea
            Spits its spume
            Upon a sandy shore
            Building, tearing, wildly,
            Fiercely free.

    That I may always show
            Compassion for a child,
            Disease-wracked
            By a thing
            He never knew,
            Or for the mindless old one,
            Child once more,
            Feebly fumbling things
            He used to do.

That I remember salty tears of pain,
    Exhausting tears
    That drain away a grief
    Leaving a soul-sad being
    Ready for
    The slow sure wisdom
    That will bring relief.

But most of all I pray
    I'll always have the taste
    For tantalizing things;
    New thoughts,
    New ways,
    For star-strewn universes,
    Beckoning light,
    For all those dawns
    That herald all the days.